Amuse Yourself in the Toilet

by Lou Rolls

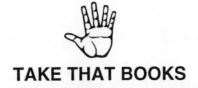

TAKE THAT BOOKS

Take That Books is an imprint of
Take That Ltd.
P.O.Box 200
Harrogate
HG1 4XB

Written by Mogul
Illustrated by Clyde

10 9 8 7 6 5 4 3 2

ISBN 1-873668-55-4

Layout and typesetting by
Impact Design, P.O.Box 200, Harrogate, HG1 4XB.

Printed and bound in Great Britain.

JUGGLE YOUR ROLLS

1.   Take one new toilet roll from the pack. If its absence is noticed, blame the damned puppy from next door.

2.   With the roll in your left hand, sweep it down past your belly button, and throw it in a smooth arc up to your right hand.

3.   Now take a second roll from the pack. Hold one in each hand. As in (2), sweep your left hand down and throw the roll in an arc towards your right hand. Just as the roll reaches your right hand, drop the one you are holding and catch the flying roll.

4.   Repeat the process from (3). This time throw the roll from your right hand rather than dropping it. For now, it doesn't matter where you throw the roll.

5.   The big one! Throw the left roll as above. Then, just as the roll begins to fall towards your right hand, sweep your right hand down past your belly button and throw the right roll in an arc towards your left hand. Catch the left roll with your right hand, and the right roll with your left hand. You may need to repeat this step several times until you feel comfortable. Remember, you should be tossing your rolls from near the middle of your body, and catching out to the side.

6.   Pick up a third roll. Say, "Darling, he's at it again." Hold two rolls in your left hand and one in your right. Now, repeat step (5) totally ignoring the third roll.

7.   Repeat step (6), but throw the third roll anywhere when you catch the second roll.

8.   As in (7), but this time, throw the third roll towards your right hand.

9.   Prepare to juggle! Repeat (8), but toss the third roll instead of throwing it. As the roll falls towards your right hand, throw the roll you are holding in that hand towards your left hand. catch the roll and throw the one in your left hand. Catch the roll and throw the one in your right hand. Catch the roll and throw the one in your right hand. Catch the roll and throw.... etc.

WARNING *Juggling toilet rolls can be dangerous in confined spaces. Never attempt to juggle while you are 'doing your business'. Think of a good excuse for your banging and clattering as you learn the basics.*

DODGY DEFINITIONS

Noah — Person who knows a lot.
Seesaw — Observer with a tense problem.
Genius — Clever Genie.
Aurora — A lion.
Moscow — Non-rolling bovine.
Vancouver — Tarpaulins for vehicles.
Bangkok — Ouch.
Brussels — Vegetating European politicians.
Kuwait — Long line of people.
Andes — On the end of your wristes.
Reefs — Laid at the cenotaph.
Consonants — Africa, America, Asia, Europe and Australasia.
Insects — Carried by the Three Kings.
Debate — Something used in fishing.
Magnet — Found in old apples.
Dusk — Found on top of shelves.
Fjord — Scandinavian car.
Gulf — Middle Eastern car.
Cyclone — Lonely biker.
Cuckoo — Surprised chef.
Feminine — Girl between eight and ten.
HiFi — Radio on a shelf.
Germ — Someone from the Bundesrepublic.
Father — Not there yet.
Uncle — Joins your foot to your leg.
Auntie — Evening meal for an aardvark.

ROOOAAARRRR

DRIVING ROUND IN CIRCLES

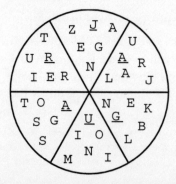

Six names of cars are hidden in this circle. Each make has six letters and one letter appears in each segment in a strictly clockwise direction. The first letters of the names also appear in different segments. Can you find the six cars? We've found the first one, Jaguar, for you. Answers on page 62.

Famous Toilets - Part 1

Neil Armstrong

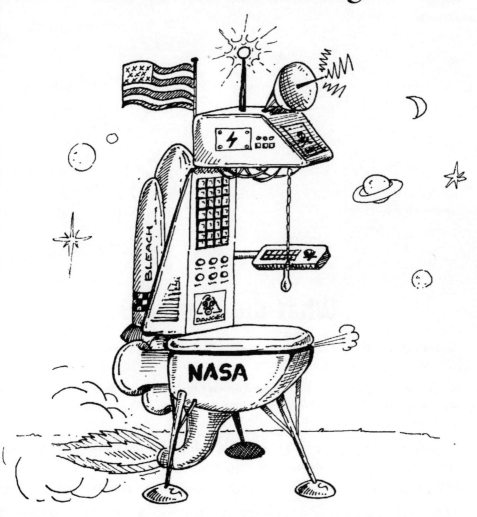

"At this height, one small dump from a man, can make an awful mess on mankind"

PHANTOM WITHDRAWALS

All may not be what it seems on your bank statement. Perhaps a ghost has been helping itself to your hard earned cash! But would you notice? Test yourself by seeing if you can spot the six differences between these cartoons. You'll find the solution on page 62.

What did you say?

"I don't give a shit what happens" - President Richard Nixon (recorded on tape and played during the Watergate investigations).

"Pass a law to give every whinging Pommie his fare home to England. Back to the smoke and the sun shining ten days a year and shit in the streets. Yer can have it." - Thomas Keneally, Australian novelist.

"You know whatta you do when you shit? Singing is the same thing, only up!" - Enrico Caruso, Italian opera tenor.

"Fish fuck in it" - William Fields, actor, giving his reason for not drinking water.

"They fuck you up, your mum and dad. They may not mean to, but they do." - Phillip Larkin, British poet.

Did you hear about the secretary caught stealing elastic bands? She got a long stretch.

TOILET CLEANER (MALE/FEMALE)

Owing to a particularly unfortunate accident involving a toilet which refused to stop flushing, the following vacancy has arisen in the recently privatised Local Authority Cleaning (Lavs) Department.

POSITION: Public Services Cleaner Required.

SEX: ~~Yes, please~~. Male/Female

AGE: Any, so long as still breathing.

QUALIFICATIONS:
- Knowledge of use of mop.
- Pride in a job well done.
- Must be able to scrub and wipe a toilet in 3 seconds (2 seconds after training).
- Knowledge of operation of sanitary equipment machines.
- Lack of olfactory sensitivity due to varying odours prevalent in the workplace.
- A deep seated desire to view clients of the facility from under the door of the cubicle.
- Ability to record occupancy time of client in cubicle and reprimand as appropriate.
- Knowledge of sexual habits of clients required to prevent any law breaking taking place in the facility.
- Knowledge of local weather, streets, train and bus time-tables to be able to provide clients with information required during their visit.
- Basic first aid qualification.

CLOTHING: Will be provided by the authority; Rubber gloves (yellow or pink); Transparent plastic over shoes; Flowery patterned hat; Overall (pink or blue).

EQUIPMENT: Mobile phone (for share dealing); Mop; Bucket; Supplies of cleaning fluid; Thermos flask; Bin.

HOURS OF WORK:
Flexible shifts, 8am-10pm or until 10pm from 8am.
Saturday and Sunday hours during Summer and Winter.
Tea breaks by arrangement.

PAY: Highly attractive and competitive salary up to £1.99 per hour

BENEFITS: Occupied Pension Scheme. Tips (for the horses). Ubiquitous water for making tea. Luncheon vouchers. Free toilet facilities.

"WHAT ON EARTH ARE THEY DOING IN THERE?"

Recent Government statistics show that women take twice as long as men to use public toilets. As a result long queues build up. Research from the *University of Unknownsmallamericantown* has revealed several possible reasons for the delay. See if you can arrange them in the correct order:

A. Women's bladders are larger than men's so it takes longer for them to empty it.

B. On average women wear more clothes than men and these must be removed and put back on. Men only have to pop out of a zip.

C. Women always take a friend in with them, so in fact the time taken is for two women to pee, not one.

D. Women use more toilet roll than men. This always get stuck in the machine and time is wasted getting sufficient quantities out.

E. Women have to deal with a messy monthly business which involves rummaging around in their handbags and then trying to unravel incredibly firmly sealed plastic wrappings found on sanitary items.

F. After a hard day's slog carrying the shopping and listening to nagging kids, women like to sit on the toilet for a rest and some peace and quiet.

G. Graffiti found on toilet walls is riveting. It must be read and then added to with lipstick or eye liner pencil.

H. Women eat toilet paper and this can be quite time consuming depending on how hungry they are.

ANSWER: B, A, E, G, D, F, C, H.

Sign in a Shop Window...

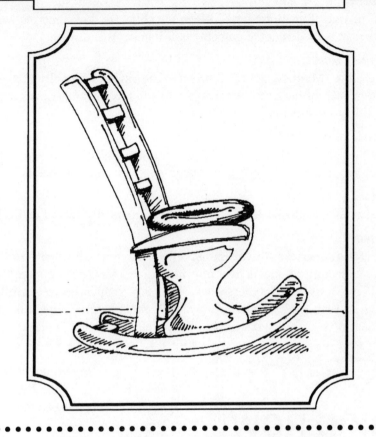

ORIGINAL ORGASM

The first orgasms experienced by women are ranked thus:

1) Masturbation — 41%
2) Intercourse — 26%
3) Heavy petting — 25%
4) Dreams — 2%
5) Homosexual experience — 1%

The first orgasms in males are produced by:

1) Masturbation — 77%
2) Intercourse — 10%
3) Dreams — 10%
4) Heavy petting — 3%
5) Spontaneous — 1%

Did you know?... *In Scotland, if someone knocks on your door and asks to use your toilet, you are legally obliged to let them do so!*

WHY DO WE SAY THAT?

"When the chips are down"
Refers to betting chips in roulette. When the chips are down and the ball is still rolling, the bet is made but the outcome is still unknown.

"Salt of the earth"
From the bible (Matthew 5:13). Curiously the saying originally meant people described as 'salt of the earth' were meant to add flavour to things as opposed to simply being good fellows.

"Fate worse than death"
Originally referred to rape or the loss of virginity outside marriage in the days when such an occurrence would have really seemed worse than death.

"As pleased as Punch"
Mr Punch as in 'Punch and Judy', has a smile permanently carved on his face.

"Geronimo"
From the North American Apache Indian called Geronimo who died in 1909. When being chased by army troopers over hills in Oaklahoma, Geronimo jumped over a sheer cliff into a river still on horseback. The army troopers dared not follow him. Years later, during the second world war, US paratroopers adopted the shout to remind themselves to talk a deep breath when jumping from the plane.

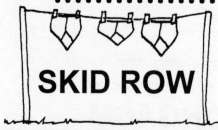

SKID ROW

A British traffic policeman's reputation went DOWN THE PAN when he stopped and challenged the late great racing driver Ayrton Senna. "Who do you think you are?" asked the policeman, "Nigel Mansell?"

The term 'skid row' has nothing to do with a washing line full of dirty underwear. No, this term started out as a phrase used by lumberjacks in Seattle. Chutes were constructed on hillsides for the logs to be sent down to the sea or to a river. Various drunks and tramps often slept in the gutter at the end of the chutes, and these areas became known as 'skid row' after the logs skidding by.

● In 1987 Australia beat New Zealand 58-0 in a world championship ice hockey game.

● The first flight by the Wright brothers was shorter in distance than the wingspan of a modern jumbo jet.

A TALE OF TEN CITIES

Hidden in this word grid are the names of ten British cities. The letters always appear in a straight line and can be horizontal, vertical or diagonal. See if you can find them, then turn to page 62 for the answers.

M	A	N	C	H	E	S	T	E	R	T	E	U	I	O
I	H	O	R	F	H	K	B	F	J	O	O	O	J	K
R	F	R	L	O	T	S	I	R	B	Y	W	G	F	M
J	U	W	R	F	V	T	G	B	R	H	C	E	D	C
T	F	I	U	H	V	B	V	R	R	F	A	U	K	L
I	J	C	H	I	C	H	E	S	T	E	R	T	H	M
Y	G	H	R	D	X	D	E	R	T	U	D	U	O	A
P	L	M	K	I	N	T	L	R	G	B	I	M	K	H
L	Y	G	V	O	R	G	E	R	D	X	F	W	A	G
U	O	J	D	F	H	M	E	T	L	G	F	T	L	N
U	Y	N	N	B	V	C	D	D	F	G	H	A	K	I
O	O	D	D	O	N	R	S	F	T	U	S	O	P	M
L	M	N	B	O	F	Y	H	O	J	G	E	F	B	R
P	I	U	Y	T	N	R	G	B	O	J	H	G	F	I
T	B	N	M	V	F	H	T	W	Z	C	E	Q	A	B

"There are passages of Ulysses that can be read only in the toilet if one wants to extract the full flavour from them"

- Henry Miller, US novelist talking about James Joyces' work

What do you get if you throw a piano down a mineshaft? A flat miner.

WHAT GOES 'DOWN THE PAN' AROUND THE WORLD?

The rubbish coming from peoples homes, shops and offices is termed 'solid municipal waste'. Most of this is simply dumped on land or in the sea, although some governments discourage the latter. This is how many THOUSANDS of tons of solid waste are produced by 'developed' countries...

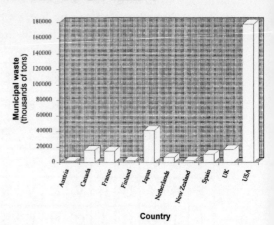

Sewage, the stuff flushed down millions of pans every day, is termed 'oxidisable waste'. Some of this is treated with mechanical or biochemical methods, but a lot of it is discharged straight into inland rivers and streams or into the sea. These are the number of tons of sewage discharged by 'developed' countries per head of population...

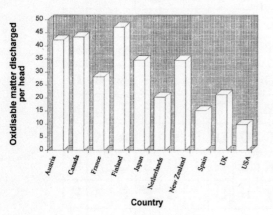

Did you know...

- You spend half and hour each day with your eyes closed blinking.
- The Dodo became extinct in 1681.
- The Passenger Pigeon became extinct in 1914.
- The first astronaut was Yuri Gagarin.
- There are only four basic types of finger print - arch, loop, whorl and composite.

GREAT TOILET ACCIDENTS OF OUR TIME
Number 59246
Explosive Bend

On 22nd July 1949, Albert Noble arrived at work full of joy. The time had come to test his new patented invention - a device for clearing blocked toilets. With the world's press gathered around, Albert stuffed his work's loo with rolls of paper, four years worth of sanitary towels and prams full of nappies. Sure enough, when the handle was pulled, water spilt out all over the floor.

Asking everybody to move back, Albert produced his new invention. Four pounds of plastic dynamite as an initiation device for three gallons of nitro-glycerine were tied with blue string (sourced from the unused sanitary towels) to an old broom handle.

Carefully, Albert placed his device into the pan next to the blocked U-bend. Pressing the red button, he winked at a particularly pretty female reporter. And that was the last anyone ever saw of Albert. An explosion equal to the force of six nuclear bombs erupted from the toilet, taking Albert to that great lavatory in the sky. Subsequent investigations revealed the towels had expanded so rapidly, they had compacted the disposable nappies below their critical size. As everybody knows, disposable nappies are not really disposable, and the resultant mulch took on a previously unknown chemical composition. Today, this material is used as a protective layer on the outside of the space shuttle.

A search for part of Albert was instigated and continues to this day. Anyone who finds a bit is awarded a Noble Piece Prize.

Doctor, Doctor

"Doctor, doctor, I think I'm a toilet"
"Don't worry, you're only a little potty"

"Doctor, doctor, I think I'm a spoon"
"Come on man, stir yourself"

"Doctor, doctor, I can't stop lying"
"I don't believe you"

"Doctor, doctor, I think I'm a tie"
"Get knotted"

"Doctor, doctor, I think I'm a snooker ball"
"Get to the end of the cue"

"Doctor, doctor, people keep ignoring me"
"Next!"

"Doctor, doctor, I feel like a pair of curtains"
"Pull yourself together"

"Doctor, doctor, I think I'm a dog"
"Sit boy"

"Doctor, doctor, I think I'm a sheep"
"Open your mouth and say, 'baaaah'"

UNFINISHED SEQUENCES

It may take an absolute genius to complete The Unfinished Symphony, but you don't have to be that smart to complete these sequences. That's not to say they are easy. You will have to think laterally as well as logically. Answers on page 62.

Sequence 1:	A	A	B	B	C	C	D	?
Sequence 2:	1	1	2	3	5	8	13	?
Sequence 3:	O	T	T	F	F	S	S	?
Sequence 4:	1	8	27	64	125	216	343	?
Sequence 5:	J	F	M	A	M	J	J	?
Sequence 6:	1	1	3	7	15	31	63	?
Sequence 7:	M	T	W	T	F	S	?	
Sequence 8:	1	2	3	5	7	11	13	?

Famous Toilets - Part 2
Noah before the flood

"I really should get this stopcock fixed."

• • • • • • • • • • • • • • • •

A*fter fifteen years of marriage, Mr & Mrs Hill fell on hard times. No matter what they did, they could not make ends meet. The phone had been cut off, there was no electricity and in three weeks bailiffs were coming to take the furniture.*

In desperation they decided the good-looking Mrs Hill should resort to the oldest profession in the world - prostitution. So, putting on as many sexy clothes as possible, she kissed her husband goodbye and went out the door telling him not to stay up.

At five in the morning, Mrs Hill arrived back at the house. Unable to get back to sleep, Mr Hill questioned his wife on how much she'd earned. "Exactly £40.25," replied Mrs Hill. Looking aghast Mr Hill said, "What miserable devil only gave you 25p?". "All of them" smiled Mrs Hill.

The Life and Times of
THOMAS CRAPPER

T HIS IS THE TRUE STORY of the inventor of the flush toilet:

Thomas Crapper was born in Thorne, Yorkshire in 1837. His father was called Chas and his mother Sarah. One of five sons, Thomas found himself working alongside his father and brothers by the age of 10 in the local ship yard Thorne Quay on the River Don.

Around this time the yards were beginning to lay people off, and employment in the local mines was also hard to find. So, at the tender age of 11 years old, young Crapper set out on a long walk to London to find his fame and fortune.

Chance brought him into contact with a master plumber in Chelsea on the King's Road. Fulfilling Crapper's desire for a job and, unknowingly, the nation's need for decent sanitation, the plumber gave him work as an apprentice.

For 13 years Crapper chipped away at the skills of his new found profession, putting in 60 hour weeks for a mere four shillings (around 20p) a week. However, the wage also included accommodation, and Crapper was given a bed in the attic of the shop - presumably not ensuite.

In 1861 the 24 year old entrepreneurial Crapper set up in business for himself at a site on Marlborough Road. In or-der to avoid direct competition with his old employers, Crapper described himself as a 'Sanitary Engineer'. Maybe it was just luck, or maybe it was a keen eye for an opportunity, but the 1860's was an excellent time to start such a business. London was in the middle of extending its very limited sewer system into a gigantic (for the time) intersecting network covering more than 80 miles.

Little more than 11 years later another turn of events worked in Crapper's favour. The Government issued a new set of regulations pertaining to sewerage in the form of The Metropolis

Water Act of 1872. This Act unified the eight separate regulations which London plumbers had been forced to work with. One of its main aims was to rectify the huge wastage of water gushing through the capital's bogs.

Enter the cistern - or Crapper's Valveless Water Waste Preventer. This patented device was advertised as having only 'one moveable part', as being 'silent acting' and as suiting 'private residences or public institutions'. At a mere 26 shillings for the up-market galvanised two-gallon version with free pull, who could resist such a device? Nobody it would seem, not even Kings Edward VII and George V. In return for their royal flushes, they issued Crapper's company with four Royal Warrants as 'Sanitary Engineers to His Majesty'. That must have really impressed the ladies!

In 1867, at the ripe old age of 30, Thomas felt sufficiently flush with cash to marry Maria Green. Unfortunately they only had one child, a son also called Thomas, who died as an infant.

This left Thomas with nobody in his family to pass his business on to. So, eventually when Thomas decided it was time to retire, he handed the company over to a Robert Wharam, who had run the business side of the company since 1867.

The world ultimately lost this great inventor at the age of 73, on January 17th, 1910.

So there you have it. If anyone ever complains at you calling your toilet 'The Crapper', you can put on your anorak and tell them the full story - and if that doesn't shut them up, nothing will.

WHAT'S IN A NAME?

Famous people have been known to dive into restaurant toilets to avoid the prying lenses of the paparazzi when they are out on the town. But can you name these famous people who simply use their real names when booking tables at restaurants to ensure anonymity? Answers on page 62.

1) Allen Stewart Konigsberg
2) Taidje Khan Jr
3) David Jones
4) Betty Joan Perske
5) Charles Lutwidge Dodgson
6) Thomas Conner
7) Lucille Le Sueur
8) Sidney B. de Millstein
9) Archibald Leach
and finally...
10) Lynda Denise Crapper

AROUND THE GLOBE

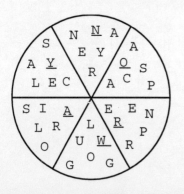

Six names of countries are hidden in this circle. Each country has six letters, and one letter appears in each segment in a strictly clockwise direction. The first letters of the nations also appear in different segments. Can you find the six countries? We've found the first one, Norway, for you. Answers on page 62.

HOW TO MAKE YOUR OWN TOILET PAPER

Toilet paper can be expensive to buy. So here are a few handy hints for all tight fisted and environmentally concerned members of the public.

1. Read your newspapers, magazines, letters and anything else made of paper.
2. Save these in a box or bin bag.
3. Cut the above into sheets measuring approximately 20cm by 20cm (no need to be exact). If you can't be bothered with squares, lay everything out on the lawn and use your mower.
4. Place the cut sheets neatly in an old shoe box or similar container.
5. Place box by your toilet or on the cistern.
6. Use as required.
7. Recycling of used toilet paper is recommended for environmental reasons. **Important: please clean the paper carefully before placing it back in the box.**
8. Wash hands and backside to remove print marks.

FLASH IN THE PAN

The five worst occurrences of lightening striking could be the following:

1) In 1697, the castle at Athlone in Ireland was struck during a severe electrical storm. The bolt started a fire in the arsenal, causing the gunpowder to explode and wipe out the entire castle and its inhabitants.

2) York Minster was badly damaged by fire when it was struck by lightening in 1984. A bishop had cast doubt on the virgin birth only days earlier.

3) An unmanned space rocket was struck while it was on the launch pad. The whole rocket and its payload were destroyed.

4) The city of New York was plunged into darkness when a storm caused a power cut. Nine months later there was a noticeable boom in births.

5) Around 44 people were injured and had to be taken to hospital when a strike hit Ascot while horse racing was taking place.

Getting the Bird

Chances are that when you pull on the toilet roll, you'll grab more sheets than you actually need. Don't let these sheets go to waste! When you've finished your business, why not have a go at making a beautiful origami bird?

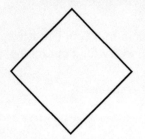

1. Take a sheet of toilet paper and crease it across the diagonals.

5. Fold in half along the short axis.

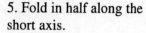
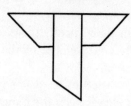

2. Fold the sheet once diagonally.

6. Fold the 'wings' upwards on both sides.

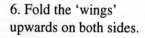
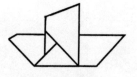

3. Fold the left corner (still 90°) towards the right side, so part of the corner protrudes beyond the baseline of the original triangle.

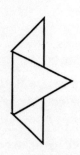

7. Take the front tip (on left) and push it downwards on the inside to produce a beak.

4. Separate the two edges you've just folded, and fold backward the top layer half-way back towards the fold made in (3) above.

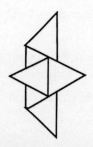

Were you born upside down? Your nose runs and your feet smell!

Famous Toilets - Part 3
Queen Victoria

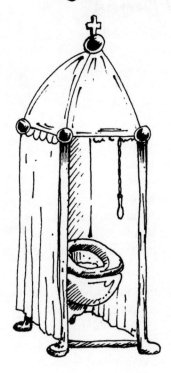

"Albert, did you leave that smell in my bog? I'm not amused you know!"

In 1603 swimming was made compulsory in Japanese schools. It must have paid off, because in the 1930's Japan were a major force in Olympic swimming events.

● After a few drinks, every woman looks beautiful.
● After a few drinks, all men are bastards.

Dignity is much easier kept than recovered.

What is the difference between a hill and the pill?
One is hard to get up and the other hard to get down.

GREAT TOILET ACCIDENTS OF OUR TIME
Numbers 61983 & 42975
Record Drops

These two accidents have been irrevocably joined in history because they both occurred during attempts to break world records. The first was an attempt at a record for the number of people on the toilet at the same time; the second was a madcap idea to go over the highest waterfall sat on the toilet.

Previous attempts at getting the greatest number of people onto the toilet had centred around how many people could squeeze into a small water closet. However, in 1962, a group of physics students decided on a new method which would produce the desired results - each person would sit (no 'h') on another's shoulders. It was a brilliant idea, each person would technically be on the toilet.

Everything went perfectly on the day. With a muscular hammer thrower sitting on pole position, 52 students climbed up to form an impressive tower. It was then that things went wrong. The edges of the seat started to give away under the strain. Apparantly one of the physics students had made his calculations while suffering from a hangover. Suddenly there was a loud crack and the seat failed. Before you could say "bail out", the hammer thrower disappeared round the U-bend. Ambulances and fire engines rushed to the scene, but in total 18 students went round the bend and were never heard of again.

At roughly the same time, Oswaldo Gonzales was preparing his 'Aqualoo' for an attempt on the Angel Falls in Venezuela. On previous outings Gonzales had piloted Aqualoo over the waterfall in his local village, over Foz D'Iguacu in Brazil and then over the famous Victoria Falls in Africa. But the Angel Falls were the big one - Gonzales was going to drop his load 979m or 3212ft. Dressed in a wet suit and wearing a crash helmet, the specially strengthened pan plunged over the edge.

For 978m of the drop, all was well. Then Aqualoo hit rock bottom. Gonzales, not having undertaken such a long 'flight' before, had forgotten to install navigation equipment. Speedy Gonzales had become Angel dust.

A few days after the D-day landings several allied troops found time to play a game of football. The match was only brought to a halt when one of the goalposts exploded. They'd chosen a land mine!

● ●

A BAD DAY

The Big Issue, a newspaper sold by homeless people in London, carried the following story. Have you ever had a day like this?

A lady went to meet an elderly relative from the Gatwick Express, a train continuously travelling between Gatwick Airport and London. Not able to find a place to park, she parked illegally. Just as she was about to get out, a policeman arrived and asked her to 'move on'. She explained the situation and was able to persuade the policeman to watch over the car for the five minutes it would take to find her relative.

In the station the train arrived on time (a miracle in itself), but getting her relative off the train proved a more difficult task than expected. Just as they were about to step onto the platform, the guard closed the door. She was trapped on a two hour round trip!

Of course, when the guard arrived, the lady had no ticket. Despite her pleas, the guard would not listen and threatened to impose a £200 fine for fare-dodging. In the end he capitulated and allowed her to buy a 'cheap' £38 round ticket.

Arriving back at the station, The two got of the train without much problem. But celebrations were cut short when they arrived at the car. A £30 parking fine had been slapped on the windscreen and a wheelclamp attached which would require £90 to be removed. Then, as if to add insult to injury, there was a note shoved under the windscreen from the policeman. It read, "People like you are the pits of the Earth. I put my trust in you and you betrayed it. You are the kind of person who makes our job intolerable."

HARD VERSUS SOFT

In the late 1970's an independent production company filmed an intellectual discussion between academics on the pros and cons of hard toilet paper. Of course, the debate never went out and the film was condemned to the vaults of the archive department. But now, Down the Pan *have resurrected this debate and produced a transcript from the original argument. The protagonists were Dr Sorewan in favour of hard paper and the French expert Dr Bébéboty who championed soft paper. Host for the evening was the ex-diskjockey Dave Le Lavis.*

Dave: Please put your hands together for our guests tonight.

Sorewan: Not so quick please.

Dave: What do you mean doctor.

Sorewan: Putting your hands together, or clapping, can transmit disease from one hand to the other.

Bébéboty: Do you mean you can catch the clap from hand contact.

Sorewan: Not exactly the clap, but more simple organisms found in excreta.

Dave: But where have these come from?

Sorewan: Germs take less than half a second to pass through two ply soft toilet tissue.

Bébéboty: That's a common statistic used by people who don't know better. Most people fold soft paper a couple of times before using it.

Sorewan: Use hard paper then you won't need to fold it.

Bébéboty: No, but you'll need ice cubes to take the inflammation away.

Sorewan: And you can use one hand. There's no need to tear the paper.

Bébéboty: What if you are left handed?

Sorewan: Pull it out with your right and pass it over!

Bébéboty: But that doesn't work for ladies who may have to hold up their dresses from the dirty floor. Are you telling me hard paper is only for men, you sexist.

Sorewan: No real man would be seen using soft paper.

Dave: Could we please leave sex out of this conversation.

Bébéboty: The only use I can see for hard paper is as tracing paper.

Sorewan: And all I can think of for soft paper is for mummifying puppies.

Dave: Steady on chaps. I just want to drop some names here, they are...

Bébéboty: I think your head is pretty vacant man.

Sorewan *(pulling chain from round Lavis' neck)*: Flush that you wimp.

Bébéboty *(throwing glass of water at Sorewan)*: Up your U-bend.

Sorewan *(grabbing handful of hard paper)*: I'm going to whup your arse.

Bébéboty: Aaarg.

At this point the security men pulled the two doctors apart. Neither party was injured but Dave Le Lavis suffered a sand-papered face and a toilet roll had to be surgically removed.

Famous Toilets - Part 4
Arnold Schwarzenneger

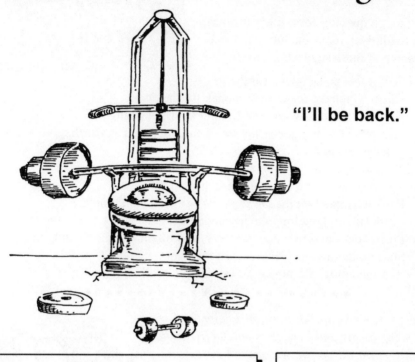

"I'll be back."

... he followed the suspects hand movements every step of the way. *Manchester Tribune.*

Wanted - babysitter, eight months old. *Houghton Advertiser.*

Wedding dress. Worn only once by mistake. Will accept $30. *Point à Pierre Hereld.*

Fats efishent typsit seeks work. *Newmacher Gazette.*

The Cats Protection League is holding a flea market in the old pump rooms on Friday. *Harrogate Shouter.*

A Plague of flies has been reported in the tiny village of Bromsly. Investigators are trying to see if there is any connection with an explosion in a trouser factory five miles away. *Pinkerrton Evening Post.*

HOW TO PASS THE TIME IN A TOILET QUEUE

Although queuing for the loo is a particularly female pursuit, men may find some of these suggestions useful...

1. Ask if this is the queue for the toilet.
2. Check you have the correct money for the door.
3. Try and do a deal with others to get the right change.
4. Ask others in the queue not to let the door shut when they've finished so you can get in for free.
5. Compliment your neighbour on her clothes/shoes/hair.
6. Tell them why you are waiting in the queue.
7. Pass judgement on the latest antics of the Royal Family.
8. Comment on how long the peroxide blonde is taking to use the toilet.
9. Pinch your child to make them cry, you might be able to jump the queue.
10. Start predicting the weather for tomorrow.
11. (For men only) Comment on last night's football match.

• •

Pierre was new to the Foreign Legion and was feeling lonely and in need of female friendship.
"What do you all do for sex around here," asked Pierre of a colleague.
"Well," replied the legionnaire, "in the desert, we have to adapt to our surroundings."
"What do you mean," said Pierre.
"You'll find out on Thursday when the camels arrive" was the enigmatic answer.
Pierre snorted and walked away - camels indeed!

By Thursday, however, he had changed his mind. Standing outside the fort, he watched closely as a cloud of sand appeared on the horizon. The cloud got bigger and bigger until he could make out a flock of camels. By now he was feeling really randy. Unable to wait any longer he rushed out, grabbed a camel and dropped his trousers.

"Private Pierre, what the hell are you doing," shouted his captain from a parapet.
"Can't you tell?" shouted Pierre, "It's Thursday and the camels are here."
"But Pierre," explained the officer, "the camels have come to take us to where the girls are!"

Problems Getting To Sleep?

Then try counting these sheep!

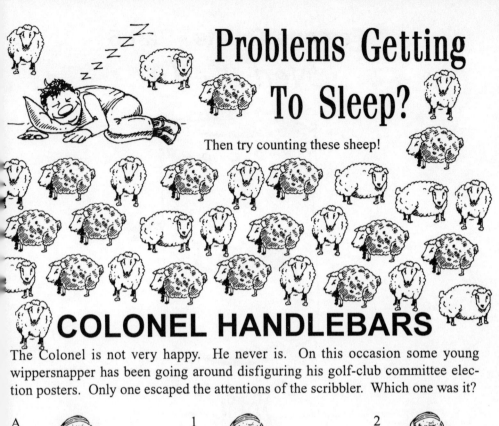

COLONEL HANDLEBARS

The Colonel is not very happy. He never is. On this occasion some young wippersnapper has been going around disfiguring his golf-club committee election posters. Only one escaped the attentions of the scribbler. Which one was it?

Famous Toilets - Part 5
Ned Kelly

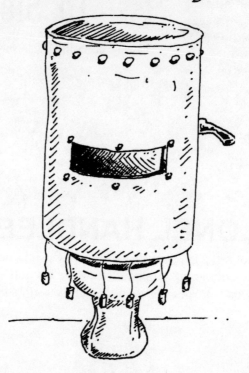

What do a team of cars do before they have a game of football? They change into their football gear!

Why do insurance companies refuse to insure cars driven by kangaroos? Because they keep jumping the lights.

There were two brothers, Frank and Dave, who always drove through red traffic lights. One day, the police spotted Frank speeding through three red traffic lights in a row. They gave chase but couldn't catch him. Just as they were about to give up, they found Frank stationary at a green light. When they asked him why he had stopped, he said, "Because Dave could have been coming the other way!"

THEY FLUSHED IT DOWN THE PAN

Some people are born rich, some achieve great riches and some have riches thrust upon them. But not many flush their riches down the pan. Here are a few reported stories of those who had it and lost it...

TOTAL CRAP

A serious *faux pas* at the annual meeting of the Society of Directors sent the jewellery chain Ratners diving for cover. Speaking to the audience, Gerald Ratner recounted how a fellow director had asked him how Ratners could sell a sherry decanter so cheaply. With a smile on his face, he proudly announced, "because it's total crap". He then went on to say one of the group's necklaces cost the same as a prawn sandwich from Marks & Spencer, but finished by saying the sandwich would probably last longer.

Ordinarily these comments would have been taken in the light-hearted vein in which they were presumably intended. But, unfortunately for Mr Ratner, reporters for several British tabloids were present at the meeting. The next day his comments were splashed across the front of many newspapers - it had been a 'low news' day.

Shareholders saw their investments drop like a bomb and soon voted for Mr Ratner to resign. The owning company was renamed to Signet and 50 Ratners shops were forced to close down, with the rest also being renamed. By 1994, the Ratners name had disappeared from the high streets.

Over a three year period, RATNERS SAW £250 MILLION GO DOWN THE PAN

TALKIE TROUBLE

B uster Keaton made his acting debut at the age of nine months when he accidentally crawled out onto the stage during one of his father's acts. This was a hit with the audience and Keaton senior, Joe, soon incorporated him into the act.

Unfortunately Joe's idea of comedy involved the beating of young Buster. This eventually lead Buster to leave his father and join the famous comedian Fatty Arbuckle, though slapstick had already been beaten into the young Keaton's psyche. Arbuckle proved a better coach and tutor for Buster, and very soon he was appearing in his first film, *The Butcher Boy*.

In the early days of Hollywood, much more expression was allowed by the actors. Here, Buster's abilities shone through. With a free reign to make it up as he went along, Buster started making his own films and formed his own production company. As the profits rolled in, Buster developed his character. His main asset seemed to be an ability to express emotion without ever smiling. Films such as *The General* set in the US civil war are still considered to be masterpieces. In 1932 Buster's income was an impressive $147,000.

Then came trouble. Talkies became the latest Hollywood fad. Soon more traditional movie moguls and investment tycoons started to appear. They made it more and more difficult for Buster by denying him the freedom he needed to be creative. At the same time, Buster's first wife left him and even renamed their three children.

After the divorce, Buster turned to alcohol. He lost his production company after several failed ventures, and had restrictions imposed on him by MGM preventing him from taking lots of work opportunities. In no time, Buster found himself in a sanatorium. In one year, his income had dropped so dramatically he had gone broke.

An income of $3,000 a week, an impressive Hollywood mansion, seven servants including a personal valet, and a partying lifestyle had GONE DOWN THE PAN.

NOT SO PRETTY POLLY

Born in Cyprus in May 1941, Asil Nadir was the son of Irfan who owned an ice cream and a newspaper business. Sent out to deliver newspapers at the age of six, Asil was soon to learn the secrets of good business.

By 1967, he had started a wholesale clothing company called Wearwell. Profits from that business, good connections in Turkey and Muslim associations allowed Asil to expand his business, renamed Polly Peck into a £12 million corporation.

Despite his success, Nadir remained preoccupied with making money and worked all hours to ensure the success of his company. By 1990, he had transformed the company into the third largest fruit dealer in the world with trading profits of £160 million. Such was his success, that anyone investing £1 in Polly Peck in 1980, would have seen a return of £120,000 in 1990.

However, The City eventually became suspicious. How could Polly Peck make so much more money from fruit than any other company? These suspicions lead to an investigation by the British Serious Fraud Office. When the news of the investigation broke, Polly Peck's shares went into free-fall. In under six hours of trading the shares more than halved in value.

Nadir was eventually charged with theft and false accounting, with allegations that £42 million had been misappropriated from his companies. Realising the hopelessness of his situation in Britain, Nadir left the country despite having been arrested and fled to his native Cyprus. Polly Peck went into receivership.

THE SHAREHOLDERS OF POLLY PECK HAD SEEN £1.5 BILLION GO DOWN THE PAN.

NO COMEBACKS

At the tender age of 15, Swede Bjorn Borg left school to become a professional tennis player. Only four years later he became the 1976 Wimbledon champion and soon attained the world No1 ranking. He became known for his ice-cool attitude and singleminded approach to the game. This focusing of his abilities allowed Borg to remain Wimbledon champion for five years.

Things started to go wrong for Borg in 1981 when John McEnroe defeated him in the Wimbledon final. This loss seemed to deal a body blow to Borg's confidence and he started to lose matches previously considered to be 'easy'. A period away from the game failed to revitalise his talent, and in 1983, Borg announced his retirement from the game.

Away from the tensions of the professional tennis circuit, Borg started upon a jet-setting lifestyle. At the same time he set up a property company called Bjorn Borg Invest, but left all the business decisions to his partners.

In 1987, he decided to expand his business interests to help fund his glitzy lifestyle. The new company was called The Bjorn Borg Design Company, and took advantage of his fame to launch a range of sports clothing. But still, he left the running of the company to others. Despite making millions in the early days, the company ran into financial trouble.

At the same time, Borg's personal life hit more rocks. His third marriage turned sour, allegedly causing him to take an overdose of sleeping pills. Within a year the design company was declared bankrupt, and other directors had decided to sue Borg for £50 million as a consequence of his continuous absence from the business.

Borg had seen his marriages, his ice-cool reputation and several million pounds GO DOWN THE PAN.

PENSION PLUNDERER

Ludvick Hoch was born in Czechoslovakia in 1923 to an impoverished Jewish family. Yet this man was to become Britain's eighth richest man before his death. He was better known by his assumed name of Robert Maxwell.

As a member of the Czech resistance to the Nazis, Maxwell started selling trinkets to earn money for food. He was forced to flee to France and eventually Britain during the war, where he joined the army and gained a Military Cross for his heroism during fighting.

After the war, Maxwell started a company for importing German scientific journals called Pergamon Press. His shrewdness and eye for a deal allowed this company to expand rapidly and soon made Maxwell a millionaire. Expansion followed with the purchase of the British Printing Corporation, The Daily Mirror newspaper and a stake in MTV Europe. His abilities seemed limitless, and the readership of The Daily Mirror soared from 200,000 to over 3.5 million. In 1990, he started the first pan-European newspaper called, simply, The European.

Little did anybody know this empire was built on fraud. Maxwell's hugely ferocious reputation kept all rumours of misdoings below the surface. Yet it is possible he realised he couldn't hold everything at bay forever. In November 1991, Maxwell fell over the side of his private yacht and drowned. Nobody will ever know if he fell or if he jumped.

With his power gone, investigators tore in the Maxwell Corporation. There they found illegal inter-company loans, huge debts, and the theft of money from pension funds. Robert Maxwell's personal fortune of £1.2 billion was discovered to be more like a liability of £1.8 billion.

A NETT DIFFERENCE OF £3 BILLION HAD GONE DOWN THE PAN.

LITTLE PEOPLE DO PAY TAXES

Leona Rosenthal was brought up in New York as the daughter of Polish immigrants. She endured two unsuccessful marriages and took up a job as a secretary in a real estate company. Showing some sort of aptitude she rose through the ranks and became a property broker.

Within a few years, Leona had set up her own company and become a self made millionairess. Her fame allowed her access to New York's society where she met and later married Harry Helmsley, estimated to be worth over $5 billion.

The lifestyle and associated power went straight to Leona's head. Her big-headedness and snobbishness became legendary. But she made one too many brags. In the privacy of her own home she told a housekeeper she didn't pay tax. "Taxes," she scoffed, "are for the little people". This statement was to later become a crucial piece of evidence in a court case for tax evasion.

A different employee left Leona's household after continuous abuse. Determined not to be walked all over by Leona, the employee went to the New York Post with allegations that the Helmsley's were claiming improvements to their mansion as a business allowance. The paper investigated the story and ran the headline 'Helmsley Scam Bared'.

Of course, this interested the tax authorities, and they soon instigated proceedings. In 1989, more than 100 former employees, many of them abused by the power crazy Leona, told of various illegal activities. The court finally convicted Leona of disguising more than $4 million of private expenditure as business expenditure, five accounts of tax evasion and of conspiring to defraud the taxman. It turned out she had thought she could avoid paying $1.7 million in taxes because she thought of herself as royalty.

Leona had seen her entire lifestyle, her reputation and personal fortune GO DOWN THE PAN.

Lowry's Toilet

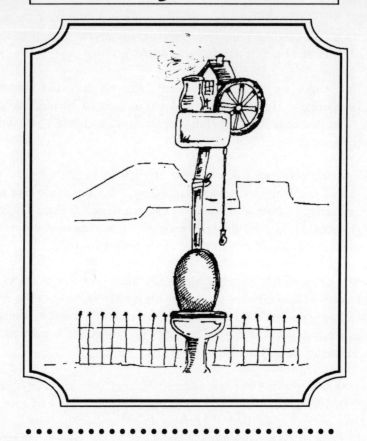

TIME WASTERS

Can you name these politicians from their nicknames? Answers are on page 62.

1. Tarzan.
2. The Ginger Whinger.
3. Cruella de Ville.
4. Attila the Hen.
5. Wedgie.

Doctor to teenage girl, "Big breaths."
Girl, "Yeth, and I'm only thixteen."

BEHIND THE BUBBLES

Hidden in this word grid are the names of ten items you may find in your bathroom. The letters of each item always appear in a straight line and can be horizontal, vertical or diagonal. See if you can find them, then turn to page 62 for the answers.

W	D	C	I	S	T	E	R	N	R	T	Y	U	I	M
D	G	I	O	L	P	L	G	I	N	G	T	K	I	E
B	T	D	H	O	K	P	Y	G	K	N	V	G	T	D
E	A	F	G	J	K	T	H	M	O	K	V	C	A	I
D	M	T	G	U	O	O	N	X	Z	Z	G	H	U	C
Y	H	J	H	K	L	I	R	E	E	S	I	N	K	I
I	T	R	E	Y	P	L	U	G	Y	G	D	R	E	N
I	A	P	H	E	I	E	R	E	F	A	K	B	U	E
O	B	M	G	I	D	T	Y	F	A	S	J	I	F	C
M	P	L	O	K	N	I	R	J	B	H	T	T	H	A
T	D	G	H	J	K	O	L	O	T	A	D	F	G	B
W	E	R	T	Y	R	U	I	O	P	K	J	H	G	I
F	G	B	N	R	M	P	O	I	U	Y	T	R	E	N
E	H	S	I	D	P	A	O	S	E	W	Q	S	D	E
F	G	M	H	J	K	N	B	V	C	X	Z	C	F	T

"Mummy, mummy, the Au Pair has left her bottom in the toilet!"
"What do you mean she's left her bottom in the toilet"
"She's left it there because she's got a disconnectable bum"
"Don't be silly darling, of course she hasn't"
"Then why did Daddy say he'd like to screw the arse off her then?"

What do you call...

A soldier laughing to himself? - Private joke

A thief in McDonalds? - A hamburgler

A blind stag? - No idea

A blind stag with no legs? - Still, no idea

A man with a car on his head? - Jack

A goldfish with a weight on its head? - Flatfish

A farmer who used to like his vehicles? - An ex-tractor fan

An open topped Skoda? - A wheelbarrow

An aardvark who's scared of ants? - A vark

A man with wires in his ears - Mike

and something a little longer...

Two Irish burglars had filled their swag bags and decided to go home early. Not having a car, they decided to steal a bus. So Paddy sneaked into the depot as Michael kept watch. Time went by and after ten minutes with no sign of the bus, Michael went in to see what was keeping Paddy.

"What's the matter," said Michael when he found his friend staring blankly at a row of buses.

"The bus which goes past our road is the number 22," complained Paddy.

"That's alright," exclaimed Michael, "We can steal a number 12 and change at Old Street!"

A BIRD IN THE BUSH

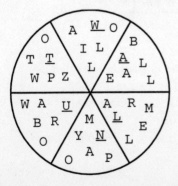

Six names of trees and shrubs are hidden in this circle. Each name has six letters, and one letter appears in each segment in a strictly clockwise direction. The first letters of the plant life also appear in different segments. Can you find the six trees and shrubs? We've found the first one, Walnut, for you. Answers on page 62.

WHY DO WE SAY THAT?

"Gone for a Burton"
Originated in the RAF during the second world war. A pilot had 'gone for a Burton' (died) when his plane was presumed to have ditched in 'the drink', meaning in the sea. A Burton drink was a strong dark ale.

"Hair of the dog"
From an old belief that fever caused by a dog bite could be cured by placing a hair from the same dog on the wound.

"Let the cat out of the bag"
Sellers of pigs at country fairs would sell an unsuspecting customer a small pig at a generous price. The pig would be placed in a bag and later handed over to the customer. Once the bag was opened the customer would find a cat had been substituted for the pig.

"Out of the closet"
A phrase originating with homosexuals in the USA who were said to hide their sexuality in the closet (cupboard). Coming 'out of the closet' was the term used when they decided to tell everyone of their inclinations.

"Make no bones about it"
A bowl of soup which contained no bones had nothing to hide.

An airline has recently started selling tickets for couples who wish to join the 'mile high club'. The plane takes off, everybody gets down to their business and then they are presented with a certificate of membership back at the airport.

In the 19th century the same people would have had a desire to do it in a railway carriage. This pastime proved so popular that many brothels offered rooms decked out like a carriage. Apparently some up-market whore houses had rooms which could be mechanically shaken and rocked just like the real thing. Helpers were employed to sound whistles and produce puffing noises.

Famous Toilets - Part 6
Napoleon

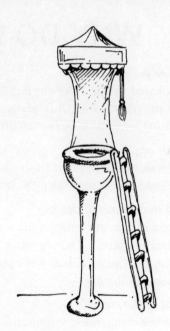

"Sorry, not tonight Josephine, I've got the runs again."

What's in a Number?

How much attention did you pay in maths lessons at school? Well, even if you'd stayed awake all the time and had a photographic memory, you'd probably not know these numerical facts...

- The sum of the divisors of 70 is a square number - 144!

- 15 is the first product of two prime numbers.

- The number 9 is written as 100 in base 3.

- Powers of 2 appear more frequently in mathematics than any other number.

- The number 371 is the sum of the cubes of its digits.

- 13^2 and 14^2 have the same digits, 169 and 196 respectively.

- 25 is itself a square number and the sum of two squares.

- Graham's number is the largest number possible - far larger than the total number of particles in the Universe.

- 1,111,111,111 is the smallest possible ten-digit Kaprekar number (its square can be summed to equal the original number).

- To the ancient Babylonians, zero (0) was simply a missing number. They wrote 23 and 203 in the same manner with notation between the 2 and the 3 to indicate something was missing!

BECOME A MASTER OF THE BOG BRUSH

Have you been doing the various puzzles in *Down The Pan*? If you have completed more than three and got the correct answers (check on page 62), then you may apply for a respected academic qualification - The Master of the Bog Brush! Each certificate is unique and proudly displays your name (or the name of a friend). They are printed on quality marbled paper.

This is to certify that

YOUR NAME PRINTED HERE

has been awarded the distinguished honour of

Master of

The Bog Brush

(M.Bog.)

after passing Hard Things in the toilet, such as irrelevant questions. Never again let it be said that this person *probably* has 'shit for brains'. This certificate is absolute proof that they do.

Signed this day _____

Lou Rolls

Author of Down The Pan

To receive your certificate - in your own or anybody else's name - write your details on the coupon or on a plain piece of paper and send it together with stamps to the value of £1.50 towards postage and packing, to:

Master of the Bog Brush, Take That Ltd., PO Box 200, Harrogate HG1 4XB.

YES, I have spent many hours studying Down The Pan, drunk a lot and generally lazed around (just like a real student). Therefore I am qualified to receive **The Master of the Bog Brush** certificate.

Please make out a certificate in the name of: _____

(block capitals) **and send it to:**

Name: _____

Address: _____

_____ Postcode: _____

Please return to: **Master of the Bog Brush, Take That Books,**
P.O.Box 200, Harrogate, HG1 4XB

ON THE CARDS

Sitting on the toilet is a perfect place to practice card tricks. Not only do you have time to CONCENTRATE, but you are almost guaranteed not to be interrupted and your technique EXPOSED. Of course, it could be a bit of a tight SQUEEZE when you come to ENGAGE your audience, but keep a dead PAN face and you'll be alright on the night.

The Four Burglars

This trick is performed to the story of four burglars (Jacks). You show your audience the four culprits in a fan. They can only see the four Jacks, but behind the back-most Jack, you are hiding three other random cards.

You tell those watching that the Jacks have decided to pull one of their largest jobs on a large office block. To do the dirty deed, they have hired a helicopter and land on the top of the office block (the rest of the cards). You should place the four Jacks and the three other cards on top of the pack as you tell this part of the story.

Tell everybody that the first Jack is sent down into the basement to see if there is anything of interest. As you do so, take the top card and place it near the bottom of the pack. Your audience will think you have taken one of the Jacks, but it will be the first of the three hidden cards in the fan.

Repeat the action, saying the second burglar goes to the ground floor to clear out the days takings. Move the second card to the middle of the pack. Then say the third Jack goes to the first floor to open the safe. Take the third card and place it in the top quarter of the pack.

Explain that someone has to stay on the roof to act as a lookout. So you will be leaving the fourth Jack at the top of the pack, and you might even want to give everybody a glimpse of that Jack (since it really is a Jack and not a random card).

Halfway through the robbery you say the police arrive and the alarms go off. The burglars have to get in the helicopter quickly. Snap your fingers and tap on top of the pack saying, "Quick lads get out".

Slowly turn over the top card, then the next and continue to reveal all four Jacks. Your audience will wonder how you moved the Jacks to the top of the pack!

Eagle Eyes

Tell your audience that you have some of the keenest pairs of eyes in the country. In fact, your eyesight is so sharp you can distinguish fingerprints on playing cards. Nobody will believe you, so you can prove it.

Take out your pack of cards, give it to anyone in the audience, ask them to shuffle the pack as much as they want and to take one card. Once they have chosen a card, take the rest of the pack, turn your back, and ask them to show their friends while they put a strong forefinger mark in the middle of the card. While the fingerprinting is going on, take a look at the bottom card on the pack. This is your Key Card, and let's say it is the seven of clubs.

Turn back, and facing the audience cut the pack at any point. Offer the top part of the pack and ask your victim to place their card on top. You then replace the bottom part of the pack on top of the fingerprinted card. The seven of clubs will now be next to the chosen card. Give the whole pack back to your victim and ask them to shuffle the pack. It is unlikely that the two cards will be separated unless they shuffle for a couple of hours!

When they are finished take the pack and spread the cards face up on the table. Ask everybody for silence as you examine the cards for fingerprints. Take a couple of looks at your victims forefinger, making out you are looking at the print. Finally, find the seven of clubs, and select the card which would have been below it in the stack. This will be the card which had the fingerprint put on it!

Perfect Predictions

You can show your friends that you can make accurate predictions about their choice of cards.

Take any pack of cards and get your guest to shuffle them. Ask that they cut the pack into four roughly even piles, and then place them on the table. Say you need to 'get a feel' for the victim's personality by looking at the cards.

Pick up the first pile and locate two cards of the same value and, if possible, same colour, ie: the five of diamonds and five of hearts. Place one of these cards face down on top of the pile and the other on its own face down in front. Repeat this exercise with the other three piles.

Now say you are ready to make a prediction and start to shuffle the first pile. One by one move the cards from the bottom of the pile held in one hand and pass it to your other hand. When your victim says stop push over the top card instead of the bottom card. This is the matching card you chose at the beginning. Make a point of saying this is the card you have chosen and place it on top of the pile.

Repeat this action for each of the other three piles, and line up the packs with your predictions which are still face down on the table. Look at your guest and saying, "This was my prediction", turn over the single card in front of the first pile. Then say, "This is the card you chose", turning over the top card of the pile. They will match in number and colour. Similarly for the other three piles. You were right, you can predict which card they'll choose!

Late Bets

Give your pack of cards to your victim, noting the bottom card - remember, this is your Key Card. Your victim will chose a card and you ask them to place it on top of the pile. Cut the cards to place your Key card next to theirs. Give the pack to your victim for a quick shuffle.

When you have the pack back, start to turn over the cards one by one with your victim looking on. Make sure all the cards remain visible as you turn them over, so work across the table as you do so. When you reach your Key Card you know the next one is the chosen card, turn it over and remember it but keep going. Deal around another four or five cards. Suddenly stop and look at your victim. Say "I bet the next card I turn over will be your card!".

Your victim will think they are on to a winner because you have passed their card already. Take the bet and move back along the table. Choose your victims card and turn it face down on the table. The next card you turned over is indeed your victims card!

Final Countdown

Select a card, say the ace of hearts. Place this card beneath the ninth card in a deck, so the ace of hearts is the tenth down. Now, having made a big issue of your ability to locate the ace of hearts from a random dealing, hand the deck to your victim. Ask them not to shuffle the pack but to think of any number between 10 and 20.

Once they have chosen a number, ask them to deal the cards one at a time onto a table, placing each card on top of the previous card until they have dealt the number of cards equal to the number they first thought of. When they have finished take the remainder of the pack and ask your victim to add together the digits of their number. So twelve become $1 + 2 = 3$, and fifteen become $1 + 5 = 6$, etc. Now ask your victim to count down that number of cards from the top of the pile they 'randomly' selected.

Ask them to turn the card over when they reach it. This card will be the ace of hearts. Stand back and take the applause.

This trick works for any number between 10 and 20. And if you can remember your school algebra, you can prove it!

Waiter, Waiter

"Waiter, waiter, this soup bowl is full of holes"
"You did ask for leek soup, madam"

"Waiter, waiter, this soup tastes foul"
"Yes, madam, this time you ordered chicken soup"

"Waiter, waiter, do you have toad in the hole"
"No maam, just a frog in my throat"

"Waiter, waiter, there's a roofing tile on my plate"
"Yes, madam, you asked for cottage pie"

"Waiter, waiter, this egg is rotten"
"Don't blame me, I only lay the tables"

"Waiter, waiter, there's a sock on my salad"
"It's only the dressing"

and something a little longer...

A man went in to a restaurant and ordered Aberdeen Steak. The food arrived but the man took one bite and called for the chef. "Chef," he said, "this steak is not from Aberdeen, kindly bring me the menu again"

The second time he ordered Dover Sole. Again, when it arrived, he took one bite and called for the chef. "This sole is not from Dover," said the man. Take it away.

For the third dish he ordered Lancashire hot pot. One mouthful into the dish, he called the chef. "Look, chef, this isn't from Lancashire," he proclaimed. Where on earth do you come from man, you certainly can't be English. "Well," said the chef, "Maybe you can tell me since you're such an expert".

Make-a-Snake

Ok, so you've pulled out far too many sheets from the bog roll, you've wasted thirty of them trying to make an origami bird, but you've still got a few left and you can't blame the puppy. So, here is something a little easier to make - an origami snake!

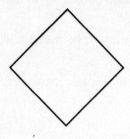

1. Take a sheet of toilet paper and fold the edges to the mid-line as if you were making a simple paper aeroplane.

2. Repeat (1) above another two times folding along the dotted lines..

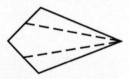

3. Fold half along the long axis.

4. Fold the left tip upwards along the dotted line.

5. Push the tip inside (like making the beak for the bird).

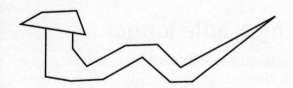

6. Repeat step (4) to zig-zag the snakes body. Make sure you leave a long tail.

Two couples got together for a New Year's meal. Just as the clock was about to strike one of the men let out a huge guff. "How dare you do that in front of my wife," said the first man. "Oh, sorry," said the second, "I didn't know it was her turn."

HOUSE TO HOUSE SEARCH

When you look in the mirror you do not see yourself as others see you. Instead, you see a laterally inverted image. Here are five possible 'reflections' of *House A*. However, only one is an <u>exact</u> reflection. Can you tell which it is?

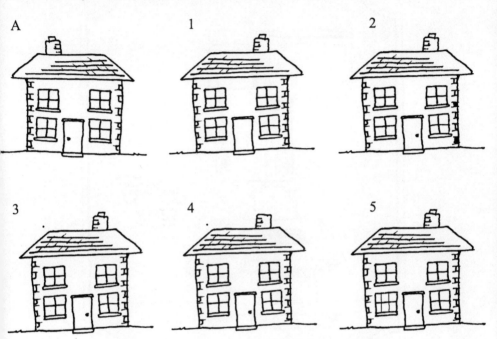

A   1   2

3   4   5

MOVING PROBLEM

A Chinese labourer went to the doctor complaining that he had constipation. The doctor gave him an examination and produced two tablets. *"Take these tonight,"* said the doctor, *"and come back tomorrow."*

Next day, the labourer returned. *"Have you moved?"* enquired the doctor. *"Me no movee. Me no movee,"* replied the labourer. So the doctor produced four tablets and told him to double the dose.

Next day, the labourer returned. *"Have you moved?"* enquired the doctor. *"Me no movee. Me no movee,"* replied the labourer. A bit surprised, the doctor produced eight tablets, the maximum dose, and told the labourer to take them.

Next day, the labourer returned. *"Have you moved yet?"* enquired the doctor. *"Me no movee. Me no movee,"* replied the labourer, *"but me movee tomollow - house full of shit!"*

Picasso's Toilet

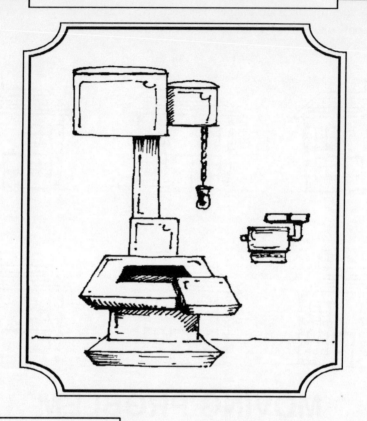

The cause of the big hole is a complete mystery. A spokesman for the police said that once the bus was removed, they'd be looking into it. *Newcastle Echo.*

All meat sold here is from local farmers killed in the village. *Sign in Butchers shop.*

The Princess is credited with saving the tramp's life. According to reports, she asked her chauffeur to call for help on her carphone. Friends say this benevolence had nothing to do with reported costs to taxpayers of the Princess' colonic irrigation. *National Daily.*

CELESTIAL BODIES

Hidden in this word grid are the names of ten planets and one satellite that can be found in the solar system. The letters always appear in a straight line and can be horizontal, vertical or diagonal. See if you can find them, then turn to page 62 for the answers.

Q	D	F	G	J	P	L	J	Y	B	J	N	K	Y	E
A	S	D	F	U	R	A	N	U	S	G	H	J	K	A
G	T	U	O	P	G	N	J	K	L	M	N	B	V	R
C	X	Z	A	I	S	D	F	M	A	R	S	G	H	T
J	J	L	P	T	O	I	U	Y	T	R	E	E	W	H
Q	X	Z	C	E	V	B	N	M	K	M	N	J	I	S
S	A	T	U	R	N	U	H	B	P	V	G	Y	T	U
F	C	V	G	F	R	D	H	J	N	L	I	Y	T	N
G	J	O	T	J	N	Y	R	E	E	R	U	T	Y	E
M	N	B	V	C	R	X	Z	N	H	G	F	T	D	V
Y	H	J	I	U	R	F	V	U	N	J	I	P	O	K
R	D	X	C	Q	S	E	W	T	P	L	M	O	K	N
U	H	R	Y	G	V	F	T	P	R	G	I	J	F	E
W	E	B	V	C	F	J	A	E	I	O	U	P	L	U
M	E	R	C	T	Y	U	R	N	U	S	N	O	O	N

"There can be few more impressive sights in the world than a Scotsman on the make"
- James Barrie

PANS ON TOUR

Hands up if you have ever suffered from "Dehli Belly", "Montezuma's Revenge" or "The Inca two Step"! Going on holiday abroad, especially to the Mediterranean regions, Africa, Asia or Latin America, is almost certain to give you a touch of stomach problems. While everybody else may be able to laugh at your antics (unless they get it too), you'll definitely have a different view on matters.

The most likely reasons for being afflicted in such a manner are:

1)   Going daft with the local food.

2)   Eating food contaminated with animal or human excreta. That means you've eaten a salad with sewage on it.

3)   Eating poorly cooked contaminated meat.

4)   Drinking unclean water. This could be in a diluted cold drink or as ice cubes. Local taps may offer little more than watered down sewage.

5)   Someone cooking the food in your hotel or restaurant doesn't wash their hands properly.

Even a Spaniard would get a bad tummy if he ate 15lb of fresh peaches!

You can try and avoid getting into trouble in the first place by:

1) Not eating food that has been left standing in the open, such as hotel buffets. Flies carry a lot of diseases.

2) Going without shellfish which may have come from polluted waters.

3) Selecting hot food. Grilled foods and fried foods are the best.

4) Avoiding salads.

5) Not eating milk or milk products such as milk-shakes if the local milk is not boiled or pasteurised.

Of course, it could be too late by the time you realise your mistakes. In this situation try to go without food for 24 hours. Get plenty of rest, and drink plenty of bottled water. Also think about taking salt tablets if you are in a hot country, since diarrhoea can lead to dehydration. Avoid alcohol, coffee and milk.

The above is only a guide, and medical attention should be sought if you have a high temperature, see blood in your stools or the diarrhoea stays for more than three days (one for children).

POTTY TRAINING

This activity usually commences when a child is aged 1-4 years. It can be a particularly stressful time for the parents. Here are some hints and tips for keeping your house in that 'just cleaned' state whilst potty training is taking place.

1. Affix the potty firmly to one spot in the house. If the child does not know where the potty is they will wee in the spot they last saw the potty.
2. Do not allow the child to empty the potty on their own. If your child trips on the way to the toilet you'll be surprised at the size of the splatter zone when his or her turd hits the wall at high speed.
3. Place a waterproof mat underneath the potty. Boys in particular do not always possess 'good aim' and there can be substantial leakage.
4. Keep large amounts of kitchen roll near the potty. This is needed for puddles and wiping the child's bottom.
5. Provide a good selection of books and toys near the potty. If your child can be encouraged to sit patiently on the potty whilst reading it will be a safer world for everyone.
6. Remind your child not to stand up to review his/her progress during usage of the potty. They will turn around and unfortunately undesirable waste may drop onto the floor. Worse, if the child turns around quickly it could be spread over a wider area.
7. Remove all toys from the path to the potty. If the child trips on the way to the potty there will be a puddle or worse in the middle of your lounge floor.
8. Keep all pets away from the potty when in use. Cats and particularly dogs, like to sniff at the proceedings.
9. Hide a pack of treats near the potty. Use this as a reward to yourself and your child upon successful potty usage.

A final word of warning. It is not advisable to tickle children when they do not have a nappy or pants on. The resulting lack of control will mean you and the furniture get very wet.

A FLUSH OF TOILETS

...or is it a Pride of Pans, a Bottom of Bogs, or a Litter of Loos?

Do you know the collective nouns for these animals? Answers on page 62.

1.	Dogs.	4.	Camels.	7.	Gnats.
2.	Wolves.	5.	Bears.	8.	Apes.
3.	Kittens.	6.	Horses.	9.	Badgers.
				10.	Whales.

Famous Toilets - Part 7
Boadicea

"Join me, and together we'll flush the Romans out of here!"

STINKING LAW

Only in America! This windy story was reported by Time Magazine.

Tom Morgan issued proceedings to sue his work mate Randy Maresh for $100,000. Maresh, he claimed, was assaulting him with flatulence. According to Morgan, his friend would hold his farts in, walk in a funny manner so as not to let it out, and then release it in Morgan's vicinity.

Maresh's attorney claimed the spontaneous eruptions were a form of free speech and therefore covered by the American First Amendment. Morgan's attorney countered that the whole affair was causing severe mental stress to his client. The judge, however, refused to listen to either side and threw the case out of court saying there was no law directly covering the discipline of flatulence.

WHY DO WE SAY THAT?

"As sick as a parrot"
More often than not associated with football managers. But the likely origin is from 1973 when several humans died of psittacosis (parrot fever) in West Africa.

"It's raining cats and dogs"
When street drainage was very poor, heavy downfalls would produce widespread flooding. When the waters cleared, drowned cats and dogs could be found in gutters and at the side of the street. This lead people to believe it had been raining 'cats and dogs'.

"He's kicked the bucket"
From people who committed suicide by hanging a rope around their neck while standing on a bucket. Kicking the bucket away would produce the 'desired' result.

"Back to the drawing board"
A cartoon in the 1940's New Yorker newspaper showed an engineer walking away from a plane crash with drawings under his arm using this phrase.

"Getting down to brass tacks"
Brass tacks were placed a yard apart in old material shops. During the haggling process, when a customer reached the stage of using the brass tacks to measure their material, it meant they were serious about the purchase.

"Excuse me!"

HUNG LIKE A WHALE

A whale's penis can reach up to ten feet in length. Each testicle can weigh around 100lbs and be 70cm in diameter.

In certain parts of France, it is still illegal to call your pig Napoleon!

What did you say?

SEX

Too many cooks spoil the brothel - Polly Adler.

Sex is like money - very nice to have but vulgar to talk about - Tonia Berg.

There will always be a battle between the sexes because men and women want different things. Men want women and women want men - George Burns.

In America sex is an obsession, in the rest of the world it is a fact - Marlene Dietrich.

Sex appeal is fifty-percent what you've got, and fifty-percent what people think you've got - Sophia Loren.

Many are saved from sin, by being so inept at it - Mignon McLaughlin.

That woman can speak eighteen languages and she can't say 'no' in any of them - Dorothy Parker.

Loop before you leap - Family Planning slogan in India.

DRINK

When it came to writing about wine, I did what almost everybody does - faked it - Art Buchwald.

The French drink steadily and kill themselves, The British drink in bouts and kill their neighbours - Bill Sanders.

I often sit back and think 'I wish I'd done that', and find out later that I already had - Richard Harris.

I'm only a beer teetotaller, not a champagne teetotaller - George Bernard Shaw.

Freedom and Whisky gang thegither - Robert Burns.

POLITICS

You four-eyed git, I'll see you outside - Tony Banks in the House of Commons.

Only one person in the world alters the vote of an MP, his wife - Joe Ashton.

It is important never to commit yourself in politics to anything that is utterly indelibly factual - Francine Gomez.

It was not a defeat, I was merely placed third in the polls - Bill Pitt.

Anybody who enjoys being in the House of Commons probably needs psychiatric help - Ken Livingstone.

GREAT TOILET ACCIDENTS OF OUR TIME
Number 17394   *Siberian Shivers*

The first Trans-Siberian railway journies were undertaken by particularly hardy fellows. Sanitation was not exactly up to first class hotel standards. In fact, the toilet was a small hole in the ground and a couple of foot plates.

This all changed in the 1940's when the first real toilets were installed for the comfort of the 'soft class' passengers. No expense was spared and rare metals were used in the construction of the seats. Gold was used for the chain and the toilet roll holder was made from aluminium. Several Kings and Queens are said to have made the long journey and praised their new found comfort.

That was until one winter's journey in the third week of January. Short of staff, the railway company had resorted to employing locals. Being Siberians they were not too familiar with the latest technology. Still, when Mikhale triggered the emergency shut down switch on the heating circuit, nobody thought of the consequences.

In the fifteen seconds it took to start the heaters again, ice cold winds blew the wrong way up the toilet ducts and hit the unfortunate occupants. Within seconds the temperature had plunged to -45°C. All metal fittings, being good conductors of heat, froze instantaneously. Hands, bums and any other pieces of flesh in contact with the toilet were frozen solid.

As rescuers broke down the doors to remove the bodies, various appendages dropped from the male bodies. This prompted a saying still in use today - "It's cold enough to freeze your bollocks off!".

Dans Le Lapin

Monsieur Desparéte arrive outside une bog occupé. Il frappe on the door.

"Allo, combien de minutes will you be"

"Pas beacoup, Monsieur. J'ai finit mais mon cherry est perdu. C'est gone."

"Votre cherry?"

"Oui, pendant ma wee, ma pendant cassé et le cherry petit dropped off"

"Bien. Je suis bursting."

Quelque minutes se passer avec much scratching et banging.

"Ça va Madam?"

"Non, ma cherry avais dissaparu"

"Est-ce par terre?"

"Non, j'ai cherche everywhere"

"Est-ce caught up dans votre vêtements"

"Peut être, mais J'ai so many. Je vais enlever tous mes bits"

Monsieur Desparéte sont trés desparet, et il frappe louder sur le door.

"Let moi vous aider"

Suddenly il frappe trop dur et le door give away.

"Ooh monsiuer, vous étes trés forward."

"Qu'est-ce que ça?"

"Qua?"

"La. C'est une pussy n'est pas?"

"Non. Silly. C'est mon lapin"

"Pourquoi avez vous un lapin dans le bog."

"Il est mon pet. C'est vrai isn't it Poopoo."

"Bon. S'il vouz et Poopoo would m'excuse. Je voudrais un peepee pronto."

"Merde"

"Non, un peepee"

"Oui, un peepee. J'ai dit 'merde' parce-que ma cherry est perdu"

Monsieur Desparéte spots quelquechose under le lavabo

"Regard, Poopoo avais poopoo au dessous le peepee WC"

"Et viola, ma cherry est dans le shit"

Stains appear sûr les pantalon de Monsieur Desparéte

"Tous le temps vous cherchez it was dans le lapin"

Madam spots les stains

"Quick Poopoo, on depart, cette homme est un drôle d'oiseau!"

Leonardo da Vinci

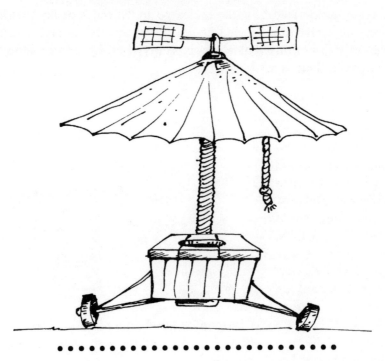

N ewly marrieds Jake and Sarah hit on a new way to save money towards their dream home. Each time they had intercourse they would put some money into the piggy bank.

"Every time we have sex," said Jake, "I'll put in £1 and next month you put the money in."

Sarah agreed and they got down to the serious business of growing their assets.

At the end of the month they both decided to open the piggy bank and see how they were doing. Jake took a knife to the base and pried it open. Shaking it over the table, ten £1 coins dropped out along with a couple of £5 and £10 notes. Jake scratched his head.

"Where on earth did they come from," he said, "I was only putting in £1 each time we screwed!"

"So," retorted Sarah "do you think everybody is as stingy as you?"

Excuses For
GOING TO THE BOG

Have you ever noticed how the ladies go to "spend a penny" while men have to be a bit more explicit about the reasons for going? Here are a few different expressions that are commonly used by one or both of the sexes, along with their origins:

Excuse: *"Powder my nose"*
Sex: Female
Origin: From the British Civil War. Women members of the various militia didn't let a lack of guns hold them back. Silently, and in pairs, they would slip into the ladies loos. With the door firmly closed, both would insert gunpowder and shot up their noses (stud earrings

would be used if no shot could be found). Then, in a blaze of glory, the ladies would burst out of the bogs snorting fire. Any of the enemy standing too close to the doors would be cut down instantly.

Excuse: *"See a man about a dog"*   **Sex:** Male
Origin: From the late 19th Century. Ownership of fighting dogs was outlawed. However, a blackmarket in these animals sprung up, and operated mostly in the toilets of private clubs.

Excuse: *"Pay a visit"*   **Sex:** Male and Female
Origin: Unknown. One possibility is the Travel Tax imposed on villagers in the middle ages. In an effort to give a boost to the ailing travel industry, everybody was required to go on a certain amount of holidays or 'visits' to other towns each year. Those who could not afford the time away from their fields paid the tax in lieu of one of their visits.

Excuse: *"Shake hands with the unemployed"*   **Sex:** Male
Origin: From the great depression. Unemployed bankers and city workers were re-trained in the art of cleaning public conveniences. These services were appreciated by most of the public who would go and shake their hands.

Excuse: *"Freshen up"*　　　　　　　**Sex:** Female

Origin: Victorian times. Dumping human sewage out of the window into the street was commonplace. Everywhere stank. Everywhere, that is, except the public toilets. These were amongst the cleanest of rooms, due to everybody doing their business in the streets. So, to get a whiff of clean, fresh air ladies would periodically retire to the toilet.

Ten reasons why a cucumber is better than a man:

1) On average, cucumbers are seven inches longer.
2) Cucumbers don't get too excited.
3) A cucumber won't ask "Was I the best?"
4) You only eat cucumbers when you feel like it.
5) Cucumbers stay hard for weeks on end.
6) A cucumber will never leave you for another woman.
7) Cucumbers don't watch football when the soap is on.
8) Cucumbers will not fall asleep on you.
9) You can have as many cucumbers as you can lay your hands on.
10) You will never have to say you are sorry to a cucumber.

Ten reasons why a pint of beer is better than a woman:

1) You can enjoy a pint while watching football and cricket.
2) A pint never says 'no'.
3) A pint doesn't get fatter as it gets older.
4) You can share a pint with your friends.
5) Pints don't have mothers-in-law.
6) When you've paid for a pint, it won't come back for more.
7) A pint doesn't get upset when you get home late from the boozer.
8) A pint never has a headache.
9) You can go to sleep after drinking a pint.
10) Pints don't get pregnant.

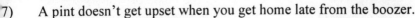

A bus full of American tourists pulled up at a camel market in North Africa. All the occupants got out and milled around taking photographs. After around ten minutes one of the tourists was getting bored. He leaned over to one of the salesmen and asked him the time in English. The Arab reached over, fondled his camel's testicles and said, "ten minutes past four o'clock".

The tourist was gobsmacked and ran over to his fellow tourists. With explicit hand movements and shouting he arrived back with the entire busload. "Please friend," he said repeated to the camel salesman, "can you tell me what the time is?". Again the Arab leant over, firmly grasped the camels balls and replied, "nearly fourteen minutes past four".

Everybody gasped in amazement as they checked the time was accurate with their watches. Fully impressed they returned to the coach. All, that is except the man who had been bored. He sensed a way to impress everybody on the bus. "Hey," he whispered to the Arab, "I'll give you fifty American dollars if you show me how you tell the time. "Okay," said the Arab and beckoned the man to sit down next to him.

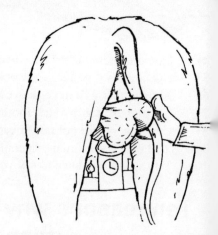

Reaching over and grasping his camels private parts he nodded forward. The American looked closely as the balls were swung to the right. "You see that clock over there," said the Arab.

Reward offered.

Missing, young dog with three legs, one ear badly chewed, blind in left eye, no teeth, fleas, occasional worms, broken tail. Answers to the name of 'Lucky'.
Stavely Post.

A HORNEY PROBLEM

If a crash of rhinoceroses was charging at you (yes, that's the correct collective term!), you probably wouldn't be too bothered about their looks. But in this identity parade, you'll see that two of the rhinos are identical twins. can you spot which they are? Answers on page 62.

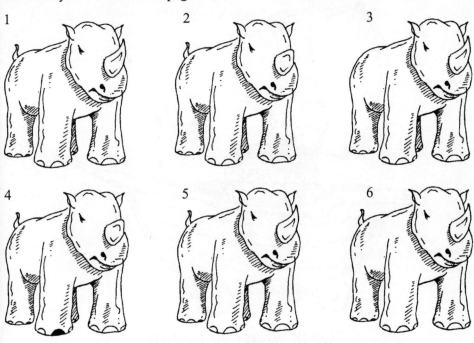

• •

A man walked into a very crowded bar in the middle of summer. It was hot, he couldn't get near the bar and he needed to relieve his bowels. Looking around, he spotted a sign to the toilets up the stairs. So he pushed his way through the crowd to the stairs. However, it had taken so long to get there that he was getting rather desperate.

Rushing up the stairs he looked around in vain for the bog. Spotting a small hole in the floor, he thought he would save time and drop his load down immediately. The relief was tremendous.

On returning back down the stairs, the man was amazed to find the bar absolutely empty. Pulling his money from his pocket, he ambled up to the bar. "Where did everybody go?" he asked. Looking up, the barman replied, "Where were you when the shit hit the fan?"

Famous Toilets - Part 6
Christopher Columbus

"Look what I've found!"

His lordship was taken to hospital suffering from hypothermia. His public diary was immediately closed, and his speech at the Refrigeration Industry Annual Dinner cancelled.
Director Magazine.

Mr Smith told magistrates he couldn't be convicted of blasphemy because he was a dyslexic and believed he was a dog.
Redburn Herald.

Ace stuntman Ted Drake said he wasn't afraid of his parachute not opening. It was the thought of the sudden stop at the bottom which terrified him.
Darlsbury Times.

Did you know?...
Protons and neutrons are made up of particles called 'quarks'.

A man was lost in the Welsh hills and dusk was drawing in. Worried that he wouldn't be able to find his way home, the man was relived to see a light in the distance. As he drew nearer, he saw that it was a very small house indeed. Knocking on the door he was met with a curt reply, "Who is it"

"I'm Brian Smith and I'm lost on," said the man. There was a pause and then the door opened. It was a young boy.

"Is your father in?" said Brian.

"No," replied the boy, "if he was in, I wouldn't be"

"Well, in that case," asked Brian, "is your mother in?"

"Of course not," said the boy, "If she was in, I wouldn't be, and neither would my father."

"In that case," persisted Brian, "do you have any older brothers or sisters?"

"Yes," replied the boy, "but they aren't in either, because I'm in."

"For heavens sake," shouted Brian, "what sort of a house is this?"

"It's not a house," beamed the boy, "it's our toilet!"

What Matters

Men think these things matter to women...

1)	Muscular chest	21%
2)	Large biceps	18%
3)	Length of penis	15%
4)	Height	13%
5)	Flat stomach	9%

But women think these things matter about men...

1)	Tight small buttocks	39%
2)	Slim figure	15%
3)	Flat stomach	13%
4)	Nice eyes	11%
5)	Long strong legs	6%

Muscular chests rated 10th, length of penis came 9th and biceps didn't figure!

Did you know?... *Large chests are considered to be terrible abnormalities in Mongolian women. All bra manufacturers have gone out of business, but the makers of paper doyleys report fantastic sales.*

DRIVING ROUND IN CIRCLES
Jaguar, Jensen, Ligier, Morgan, Suzuki, Talbot.

AROUND THE GLOBE
Angola, Poland, Greece, Israel, Norway, Cyprus.

A BIRD IN THE BUSH
Walnut, Myrtle, Azalea, Bamboo, Poplar, Willow.

TIME WASTERS
1. Michael Heseltine.
2. Neil Kinnock.
3. Edwina Curry.
4. Margaret Thatcher.
5. Tony Benn.

A FLUSH OF TOILETS
1. A Kennel.
2. A Pack or Rout.
3. A Kindle.
4. A Flock.
5. A Sloth.
6. A Stable.
7. A Cloud.
8. A Shrewdness.
9. A Cete.
10. A School.

UNFINISHED SEQUENCES
D - Simple, each letter appears twice!
21 - Add the previous two numbers.
E - First letters of one, two, three...
512 - Cube of numbers.
A - First letter of months.
127 - Powers of two minus one.

M - First letters of days of week.
17 - Prime numbers.

HORNEY PROBLEM
Rhinos 1 and 5.

HOUSE TO HOUSE SEARCH
House 3 matches House A.

A FLUSH OF TOILETS
1. A Kennel.
2. A Pack or Rout.
3. A Kindle.
4. A Flock.
5. A Sloth.
6. A Stable.
7. A Cloud.
8. A Shrewdness.
9. A Cete.
10. A School.

TIME WASTERS
1. Michael Heseltine.
2. Neil Kinnock.
3. Edwina Curry.
4. Margaret Thatcher.
5. Tony Benn.

WHAT'S IN A NAME
1) Woody Allen
2) Yul Bryner
3) David Bowie
4) Lauren Bacall
5) Lewis Carroll
6) Sean Connery
7) Joan Crawford
8) Cecil B. de Mille
9) Cary Grant
10) Marti Caine

CELESTIAL BODIES

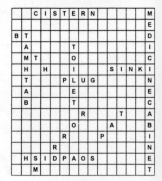

BEHIND THE BUBBLES

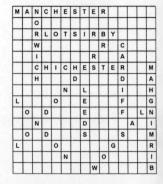

A TALE OF TEN CITIES

COLONEL HANDLEBARS
Poster 2 is the same as Colonel A.

MORE HUMOUR TITLES...

The Ancient Art of Farting by Dr. C.Huff

Ever since time began, man (not woman) has farted. Does this ability lie behind many of the so far unexplained mysteries of history? You Bet - because Dr. C.Huff's research shows conclusively there's something rotten about history taught in schools. If you do most of your reading on the throne, then this book is your ideal companion. Sit back and fart yourself silly as you split your sides laughing! *£3.99*

A Wunch of Bankers

Do you HATE BANKS? Then you need this collection of stories aimed directly at the crotch of your bank manager. A Wunch of Bankers mixes cartoons and jokes about banks with real-life horror stories of the bare-faced money-grabbing tactics of banks. If you think you've been treated badly, read these stories!!!! *£3.99*

The Hangover Handbook & Boozer's Bible
(In the shape of a beercan)

Ever groaned, burped and cursed the morning after, as Vesuvius erupted in your stomach, a bass drummer thumped on your brain and a canary fouled its nest in your throat? Then you need these 100+ hangover remedies. There's an exclusive Hangover Ratings Chart, a Boozer's Calendar, a Hangover Clinic, and you can meet the Great Drunks of History, try the Boozer's Reading Chart, etc., etc. *£3.99*

The Beerlover's Bible & Homebar Handbook
(also in the shape of a beercan)

Do you love beer? Then this is the book you've been waiting for - a tantalising brew of fascinating facts to help you enjoy your favourite fluid all the more. Discover how to serve beer for maximum enjoyment... brew your own... entertain with beer... cook tasty recipes... and more! Includes an exhaustive listing of beers from all over the world with their flavours, colours and potency. You'll become a walking encyclopedia on beer! £3.99

A Slow Screw Against the wall (& Other Cocktails)

Over 200 recipes for luscious and lively cocktails. Even the most serious of cocktail drinkers will find something new for their taste buds to savour. £3.99

The Bog Book
(In the shape of a toilet seat)

How much time do you spend in the bog every day? Are you letting valuable time go to waste? Not any longer! Now you can spend every second to your advantage. The Bog Book is packed with enough of the funny, the weird and the wonderful to drive you potty. Fill your brain while you empty your bowels! £3.99